About the Book

Whether you need a costume for a party, a play, or a holiday, you will find a costume or a method of making one that is fast and easy. Making the costume can be as much fun as wearing it. The instructions are simple and will require materials readily found around the house. Read the instructions before you begin. Collect all the materials and tools that you will need. Don't hesitate to make changes or additions.

EASY TO MAKE
COSTUMES

WRITTEN AND ILLUSTRATED BY FRIEDA GATES

HARVEY HOUSE, PUBLISHERS, NEW YORK, NEW YORK

Thank you Carol.

Manufactured in the United States of America
ISBN 0-8178-5908-X

Harvey House, Publishers
20 Waterside Plaza, New York, New York 10010
Published in Canada by Fitzhenry & Whiteside, Ltd., Toronto

CONTENTS

TOOTHPASTE TUBE

Materials: white sheet, paper bag that will fit on the top of your head comfortably, white shirt. **Tools**: scissors, pins, crayon, needle and white thread or glue, poster paint, pencil.

Tube

1. Fold sheet in half and lay it on the floor. Lie on top of the sheet. Have someone use a crayon to draw the outline of a tube shape around you. The bottom of the tube should end at your ankles.
2. Allow extra areas for seams at your shoulders and sides. Pin seams together.
3. Cut out tube shape. Cut a hole for your head to fit through.
4. Sew or glue shoulders and sides together. Make sure you leave armholes. Remove pins and turn sheet inside out.
5. Draw and paint a design on your sheet so it will look like a toothpaste tube. You can make up your own brand and design.

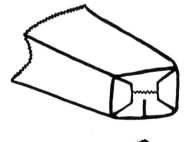

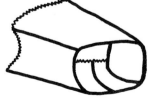

Cap

1. If your bag is too big, cut up one side and glue it smaller.
2. Fold the bottom corners of the bag inward, about 3 inches.
3. The bag-cap can be white or painted a color.

Wear a white shirt so your arms will be the same color as the tube.

CHRISTMAS TREE

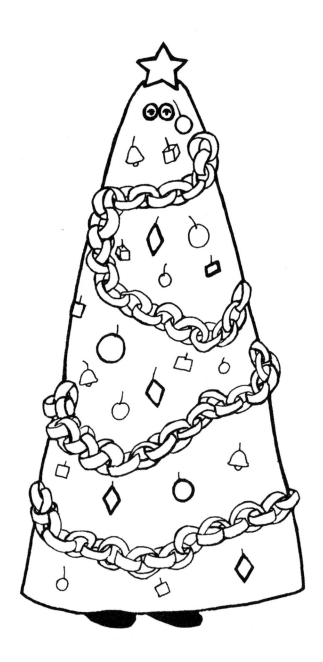

Materials: green sheet or white sheet dyed green, colored construction paper, string. **Tools**: scissors, pencil, glue or stapler, needle and thread or safety pins, crayons.

Ornaments

1. Make paper chains. Cut strips of paper 1 inch wide and 6 inches long. Glue or staple the ends together to build a chain. Pin the ends to the sheet-tree.

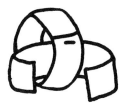

2. Draw Christmas tree ornaments, such as balls, stars, figures, and animals. Color and cut them out.

3. Pull string through the tops of the ornaments.
4. Sew or use safety pins to attach ornaments to the sheet-tree.
5. Make a star for the top. Include a base to insert in a slit at the top of the sheet-tree.

Tree

1. Place the sheet over your head. Have someone trim the bottom of the sheet, so you won't trip over it.
2. Find your eyes, mark them with x marks. Draw a small line on the top for the star.
3. Take off sheet and cut out eye holes. Make a slit in the line for the star.
4. Glue base of star in slit.
5. Decorate tree with ornaments and chains.

Small unbreakable ornaments and tinsel can also be used.
Cut up old Christmas cards for pretty decorations.

GHOST

Materials: white sheet, empty large size cereal box, small piece of dark sheer fabric, (such as a nylon stocking), string.
Tools: scissors, adhesive tape, black marker or crayon, glue.

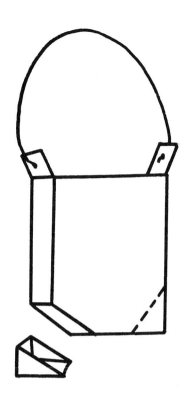

1. Cut off the bottom corners of a cereal box. Make holes in the side flaps and attach strings to tie under your chin.
2. Place the box on your head. Tie strings. Drape the sheet over you. Feel where your eyes and nose are. Mark this area with a large x mark. This is the ghost's mouth.
3. Cut around the x mark to an oval shape. Tape the sheer fabric on the inside of the sheet to cover the opening.
4. Draw a mouth around the oval shape on the outside of the sheet. Draw mean eyes and brows, and a nose.
5. Glue the top of the sheet to the cereal box. This will prevent the sheet from slipping.

Hoot and howl to sound like a ghost.

ANCIENT ROMAN

Materials: single size white sheet, white T-shirt, green construction paper, string. **Tools**: scissors, pencil.

Garment

1. Hold the sheet lengthwise and wrap it around your waist. Fold the sheet down from the top so it will reach your ankles.
2. Bring the extra length of sheet over your left shoulder and drape it over your right shoulder.

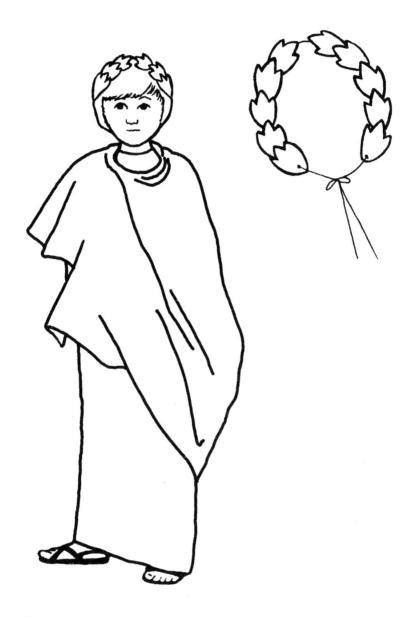

Wreath

1. Draw 8 or 10, 2-inch leaves on green paper.
2. Cut out the leaves. Make a hole in the center of each leaf.
3. Pull the string through the leaves. Place the wreath on your head and tie it at the back.

Wear sandals to complete your costume.

MAILBOX & TRASH BIN

Materials: cardboard carton*, blue shirt or sweater.
Tools: scissors, pencil, red, white and blue poster paint.

1. Cut out area large enough for your head.
2. Put box on and have someone mark comfortable armholes.
3. Cut out armholes. Cut a mail slot.
4. Letter **U.S. MAIL**, and paint the box red, white, and blue.

The same box can be a trash bin. Don't make a mail slot. Paint it green and letter **TRASH** across the front.

*The size of the carton is important. You must find one that fits comfortably, or one you can cut down and adjust to fit.

GIFT PACKAGE

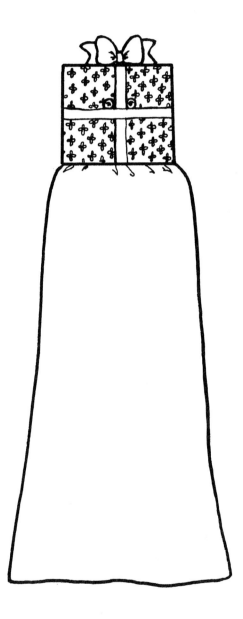

Materials: cardboard carton to fit over your head, gift wrapping paper, ribbon, fabric—wide enough to gather and fit around you, and long enough to fit from your neck to the floor.

Tools: scissors, tape, glue.

Package

1. Cut the bottom out of the box.
2. Cover and glue the gift paper on the box. Glue flaps of paper to the bottom edge inside the box.
3. Cut out eye holes and a few small breathing holes.
4. Cut part of the ribbon into 4 strips. Attach them to the center of each side, and cross them at the top. Tape on a pretty bow at the top.

Skirt

1. Fold the top edge of the fabric down about 2 inches.
2. Cut slits about every 3 inches through the folded edge.
3. Insert and pull a ribbon through the slits. Gather and tie the skirt around your neck.
4. Cut slits for your arms.

TELEVISION SET

Materials: cardboard carton, (perhaps one from a TV set) 4 plastic bottles with screw-on tops, fabric (to fit the width of the box and the length from the bottom of the box to your ankles). **Tools**: scissors, pencil, glue, stapler, black marker or crayon.

1. Cut out a television screen shape in the front of the box. Cut 4 holes where dials will be placed. The holes should be the size of the bottle necks.
2. Cut off the tops of the bottles at the necks.
3. Insert the bottle necks into the holes in the box. Screw on their tops. These are the television dials. Letter words for their use: **On, Off, Contrast, Vertical Hold, Brightness.**
4. Make 2 double strips of fabric to fit across your shoulders. Staple these straps to the edges of the carton.
5. Glue a skirt around the bottom edge of the carton. It will look like the television set is on top of a table.
6. Put the box with the skirt over your head. Now smile, you are on TV!

JACK-IN-THE-BOX

Materials: cardboard carton to fit your size, rope or twine, ribbon, a funny hat or a paper cup with strings, paper or paint to cover box, crepe paper or fabric, (45 inches long, 20 inches wide).
Tools: scissors, brush for paint or glue for paper.

Box

1. Cut the top of the box to create a lid.
2. Use rope or twine as suspenders to hold the box on your shoulders. Poke holes at front and in back of box. Tie a knot at one end of the rope and pull it through. Be sure to have enough rope to fit from your waist to your shoulders. Tie a knot at the other end.
3. Decorate the box with paint or cover it with pretty paper.

Collar

1. Fold crepe paper or fabric in half lengthwise.
2. Make holes every 3 inches at the edge of the material.
3. Insert the ribbon into the holes and pull it through.
4. Place the collar around your neck. Pull the ribbon through and tie a bow.

Hat

1. Decorate a paper cup hat.
2. Make holes on 2 sides at the opening of the cup. Knot a string and pull it through the hole on one side. Allow enough string to fit under your chin. Pull the string through the other hole and tie another knot.

Crouch in your box and pop out.

ROBOT

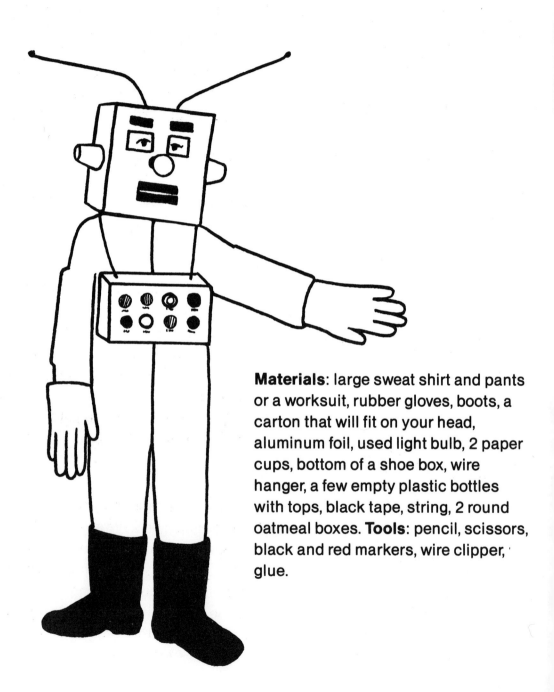

Materials: large sweat shirt and pants or a worksuit, rubber gloves, boots, a carton that will fit on your head, aluminum foil, used light bulb, 2 paper cups, bottom of a shoe box, wire hanger, a few empty plastic bottles with tops, black tape, string, 2 round oatmeal boxes. **Tools**: pencil, scissors, black and red markers, wire clipper, glue.

Head

1. Cover the head box with aluminum foil.
2. Cut out square shapes for eyes.
3. Cut a hole for the light bulb nose.*
   Fit the bulb tightly in place.
4. Straighten the hanger. Cut 2 8-inch lengths. Insert them into the top of the box-head as antennae.
   Tape on foil tips. Bend and tape the bottom ends to the inside of the box.
5. Stick on black tape around the eyes. Use tape to create brows and a mouth.
6. Tape on paper cup ears.

Controls

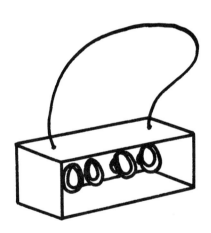

1. Cover the shoe box with aluminum foil.
2. Cut tops off the bottles at the necks.
3. Make holes in the shoe box and insert bottle necks through the holes. Screw on bottle tops. These are dials to turn the robot off and on. Other dials can be for special movements, etc.
4. Write directions on paper and glue them under the dials.
5. Poke holes on either side at the top of the control box. Knot a string and pull it through one hole, allowing enough string to go around your neck and pull it through the other hole. Tie another knot at this end.

Wear oatmeal boxes under your sleeves. The robot will look like it is jointed together.

*Christmas tree bulbs make good noses.

SUNSHINE

Materials: 1 or 2 pieces of poster board, (for a large sun, tape 2 pieces together), yellow crepe paper streamers, yellow or orange shirt and tights. **Tools**: yellow, orange, and red poster paints, pencil, string, straight pin, scissors, stapler, tape.

1. Tie one end of the string to the eraser end of the pencil. Put a straight pin through the other end of the string. Place the pin in the center of the board. Draw as wide a circle as possible.
2. Add points to the edge of the circle. Draw and paint a face on the sun.
3. Draw and cut out eye holes at the top of the sun face. Cut out sun face.
4. Cut streamers in varying lengths. Staple streamers to the points.
5. Cut 2 poster board strips, 1 inch wide and 8 inches long. These are handles.
6. Tape handles in comfortable places on the back of the sun.

You can make up other easy costumes using this method.
How about a cloud with crepe paper or plastic rain?
You can make a target with a paper arrow stuck in the bull's-eye.
Think of some more ideas.

SHOPPING BAG BIRD

Materials: a large shopping bag with the handles cut off, 3 large grocery bags, a small bag that will fit over your head comfortably, 3 pieces of yellow construction paper or paper plates, colored yellow, tan or brown tights, yellow or orange knee socks.
Tools: scissors, crayons or markers, glue, tape.

Body, wings and tail

1. Cut a slit up the back of the shopping bag. Cut a neck hole at the bottom. Cut armholes on each side. For a taller bird, glue another bag to the bottom of the body bag. Use tape to hold the body bag together when you wear this costume.

2. Cut openings at the bottom and into the back of the 2 grocery bags. These are sleeve wings. The sleeves can be taped to the body bag at the shoulders.
3. Cut a tail shape from the third grocery bag. Tape the tail in place after you put on the body bag.
4. Draw feathers with crayons or markers.

Head

1. Place the small bag on your head. Feel and mark places for eye holes. Take off the bag and cut out eye holes. Shorten the bag so it fits to your neck.
2. Cut a beak shape out of yellow paper. Glue beak in place. Decorate eyes.
3. Cut 2 strips of yellow paper. Curl and glue them on top of the bag.

Alternate Head

Cut a hole for your face in the paper bag. Make a beak out of yellow paper or a paper plate. Tie the beak on with strings attached to each side.

Feet

Cut feet out of yellow paper or plates. Tape them together at the back of your ankles.

CORN ON THE COB

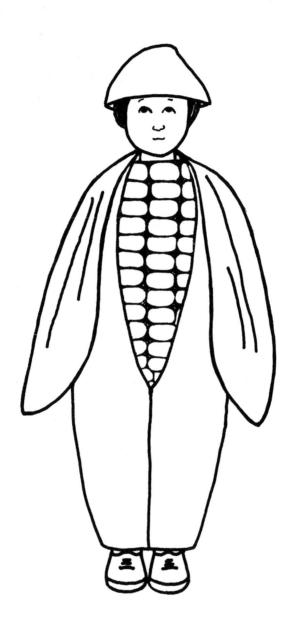

Materials: 1 sheet of poster board, 2 packages of green crepe paper, green shirt and pants or tights, ribbon or cord (enough to fit around your waist). **Tools**: scissors, pencil, yellow paint, stapler, tape.

Cob

1. Measure the width of your chest and the length from your neck to thighs.
2. Using these measurements, draw a corncob shape on poster board. Add pieces at the waist to hold ribbon.
3. Draw and paint kernels on cob.

Husk

1. Fold crepe paper in half. Cut half of the paper lengthwise. Cut slits for neck opening.
2. Staple sides together. Leave armholes. Turn paper inside out.
3. Cut crepe paper flaps to cover arms. Staple or tape them at the shoulders.

Hat

1. Cut and fold crepe paper to a 10-inch square.
2. Staple one side closed.
3. Cut rounded shape. Turn inside out.

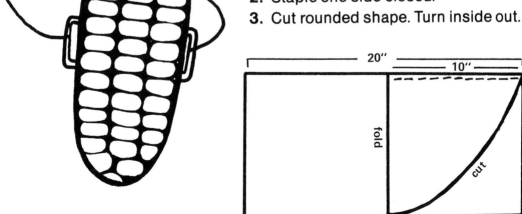

CLOTHESLINE

Materials: a friend, 2 paper bags, clothesline or cord, clothes-pins, some old clothes that can be hung without hitting the ground. **Tools**: scissors, pencil.

Put bags over your heads. Find eyes and mark them. Remove
bags and cut out eye holes. Tie clothesline around your chests.
Allow a length of line to hang clothes on. Hang up *dry* clothes.

HAWAIIAN DANCER

Materials: 1 or 2 tan or green plastic trash bags, halter or bathing suit top, red or pink crepe paper, ribbon to fit around your waist.
Tools: scissors, needle and thread, tape.

Skirt

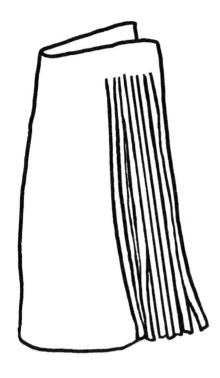

1. Cut up one side and through the bottom of the plastic bags.
2. Cut the bag into 1/2- to 1-inch strips. Leave 2 or 3 inches from the waist end of the bag. The more bags used, the fuller the skirt will be.
3. Wrap the bag around your waist. Use tape to hold it in place. Tie the ribbon over the bag around your waist. The ribbon can be decorated with sewn on buttons or shells.

Crepe paper lei

1. Cut crepe paper strips, 1 1/2-inches wide and several yards long.
2. Thread a needle and insert it at one end of the strips. Gather the paper together and twist it on the thread until it crinkles up.
3. Tie the thread ends together when the lei is long enough. Make one or several in many colors. Wear them around your neck, on your head, on your wrists, and on your ankles.

WITCH DOCTOR

Materials: T-shirt and shorts, large piece of carton cardboard, 2 or more large plastic trash bags. **Tools**: pencil, scissors, poster paints, tape, heavy string or cord.

Mask

1. Draw a large mask on cardboard.
2. Paint features and designs on the mask.
3. Cut the mask out. Somewhere on the mask, cut a hole large enough for you to see out of.
4. Tape plastic strips, cut from the trash bags, to top of mask.
5. Poke holes on each side of the mask. Tie cords through the holes to hold the mask on your head.

Costume

1. Cut openings for your head in the bottom of each of the plastic bags.
2. Cut strips 1/2 to 3/4 of an inch wide from the end of the bag to about 3 inches from the neck. The more bags used, the fuller the costume will be.
3. Use tape to hold the bags around your neck.

Cut small fringe bands for your wrists and ankles.
Tape the ends to hold them together.

"ITS"

Materials: 1 or more large plastic trash bags, leotards or matching shirt and tights, a hat, egg carton or sunglasses.
Tools: scissors, string.

Costume

1. Cut the bag into 1/2- to 1-inch strips.
2. Gather the strips and tie them together at one end.
3. Place the tied bunch of strips over your head. Be sure you part the strips so you can see. Put a hat on to hold the strips in place.

Bulging eyes

1. Cut 2 adjoining egg sections from the egg carton. Include side pieces.
2. Cut out space for the bridge of your nose. Cut holes for your eyes.
3. Poke holes and pull a string through each of the side pieces.

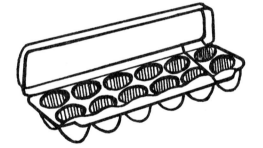

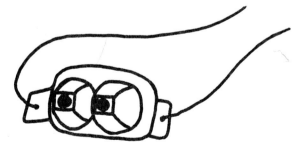

Sunglasses can be used instead of egg carton eyes.

SCARECROW

Materials: an old pillow case, large size jacket or shirt, overalls or jeans, an old hat, newspapers, scraps of fabric, ribbon.
Tools: scissors, glue or needle and thread, tape, crayons or markers.

Clothes

1. Cut newspaper into 1/2-inch strips.
2. Tape strips at the ends of the sleeves and pants. This will look like the scarecrow's stuffing is sticking out.
3. Cut patches from the scraps of fabric. Sew or glue the patches on the jacket and pants.

Head

1. Place the pillow case over your head. Feel where your eyes and mouth are. Mark these spots.
2. Take off the pillow case and cut out holes for your eyes and mouth.
3. Draw a face on the pillow case.

Tie a ribbon around your neck to hold the pillow case head in position. Put on your hat and go scare some crows.

PIRATE

Materials: striped or brightly colored shirt, pants, sash to fit around your waist, head scarf, beaded necklace, boots, brass curtain ring, black construction paper, string or black ribbon, carton cardboard, aluminum foil, a burnt cork.

Tools: needle and thread, scissors, glue, paint, pencil, tape.

Head

1. Tie the scarf on your head so that the scarf covers one ear. Take off the scarf without untying it.
2. Sew the brass curtain ring to the scarf where it will look like an earring when the scarf is worn.

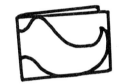

3. Draw and cut an eye patch out of black paper. Pull a string or a ribbon through it.
4. Fold a piece of black paper in half. Draw only half of a moustache shape. Cut the folded moustache out.

5. Unfold and tape the moustache above your upper lip. Rub a burnt cork on your cheeks for an unshaven look.

Sword

1. Draw and cut a sword out of cardboard.
2. Cover and glue aluminum foil on the blade of the sword.
3. Paint the handle.

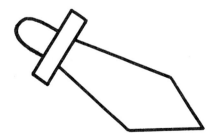

Wear the sword through the sash at your waist.

CLOWNS

Materials: large size jacket and pants, old hat, brightly colored tie, heavy yarn, a nylon stocking **OR** a large size dress, a sheet for stuffing, old hat with flowers, crepe paper or fabric 20 x 45, ribbon. **Tools**: needle and thread, scissors.

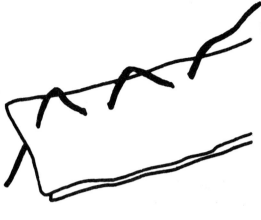

Lady Clown's Collar

1. Fold crepe paper or fabric in half lengthwise.
2. Make holes every 3 inches at the edge of the material. Fabric can be folded under 1/2 inch and hemmed.
3. Insert the ribbon through the holes and pull it through. Place the collar around your neck, pull the ribbon and tie a bow.

Lady Clown's Make-up

Green eye shadow, bright red lipstick, rouge, eyebrow pencil.

Apply eye shadow. Draw eyelash lines and brows with the eyebrow pencil. Color the tip of her nose and draw a dainty mouth with lipstick. Draw round rosy cheeks with rouge.

Use the sheet for stuffing under the dress of the fat lady clown.

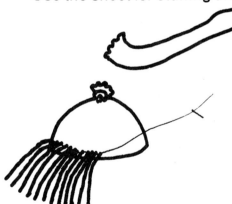

Gentleman Clown's Wig

1. Cut yarn into 15- to 20-inch lengths.
2. Knot the leg of the stocking to make a cap. Cut off the extra stocking leg.
3. Sew the yarn to the stocking cap.

Gentleman Clown's Make-up

White make-up stick, bright red lipstick, rouge, eyebrow pencil.

Use eyebrow pencil to draw heavy sad brows, small vertical lines above and below the eyes, and a large sad mouth. Fill in the mouth area with white make-up. Color the tip of his nose with red lipstick. Draw round rosy cheeks with rouge.

CAT, RABBIT, DOG, MOUSE

Materials: pajamas with feet or sweater or shirt with pants or tights of one color, socks the same color, fabric the same color, piece of pink felt or paper for a nose, broom straws, ribbon. **Tools**: scissors, needle and thread, pins, glue.

RABBIT

Use same instructions. Cut long ears out of poster board. The tail is a wad of cotton on tape and pinned in place.

DOG

Use same instructions. Cut a hole for nose and mouth. Glue a paper cup in place for a snout. Insert broom straw whiskers.

MOUSE

Use same instructions. Cut a hole for nose and mouth. Glue a cone-shaped paper cup in place for a snout. Paint the tip black. Insert broom straw whiskers.

Head

1. Fold fabric in half. Lay your head on fabric and have someone draw the outline of your head. Allow area for seams. Pin it together.
2. Cut out hood shape and sew it together. Turn hood inside out.
3. Put hood on. Mark eyes, nose and mouth. Take off the hood. Cut holes for eyes and an opening for your mouth.
4. Cut and glue on a nose shape. Sew on broom straw whiskers.
5. Cut out ears from fabric. Sew them on top of the hood.
6. Tie hood around your neck with ribbon.

Alternate ways of making the head

1. *Pillow case*: Follow instructions above from No. 3. Add paper ears.
2. *Ski cap*: Follow instructions above from No. 4. Add fabric or paper ears.
3. *Paper bag*: Follow instructions above from No. 3. Use markers or crayons to draw features. Bag corners become ears.

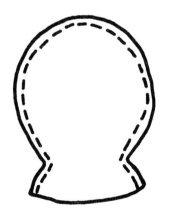

Roll fabric about 8 inches wide, into a **tail** about 20 inches long. Stitch it together. Pin it to your pants.

Paws are socks worn on your hands. A pair of boots will make you "Puss in Boots."

CATERPILLAR

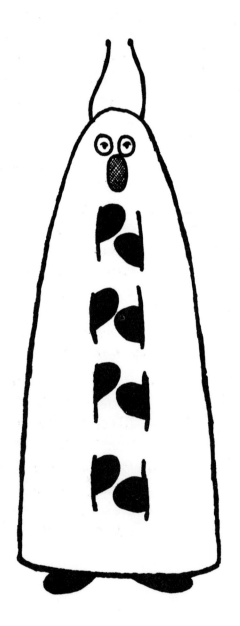

Materials: fake fur fabric, 4 pairs of socks, rags for stuffing, small piece of sheer fabric, (such as a nylon stocking), 2 small beads, long pipe cleaners. **Tools**: white chalk, scissors, pins, glue, tape, needle and thread.

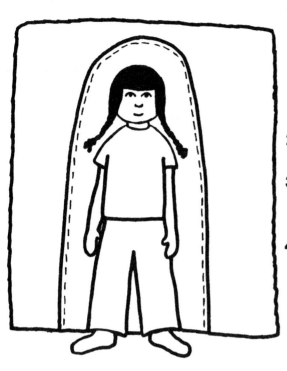

1. Fold fabric in half and inside out. Lay the fabric on the floor and lie on top of it. Have someone use chalk to draw an outline around you. The outline should be at least 6 inches away from your body.
2. Pin seams 1-inch from the edge of the outline.
3. Cut out the pinned shape. Sew or glue the seams together. Turn inside out.
4. Put on fur to find where holes for eyes, nose and mouth should be. Mark these areas with chalk. Mark slits where hands can come out comfortably in front. Take off fur and cut eye holes, one hole for your nose and mouth, and slits for your hands.
5. Stuff all but one pair of socks. Sew socks in place. The unstuffed pair are worn on your hands.
6. Cut sheer fabric to fit over the nose and mouth opening. Glue or sew it in place on the inside of the head.
7. Bend and stitch the ends of the pipe cleaners to the top of the caterpillar's head. Add small beads to the tips. Use tape to hold the beads in place.

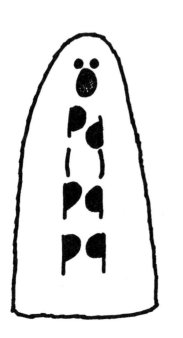

OTHER PLANET PERSON

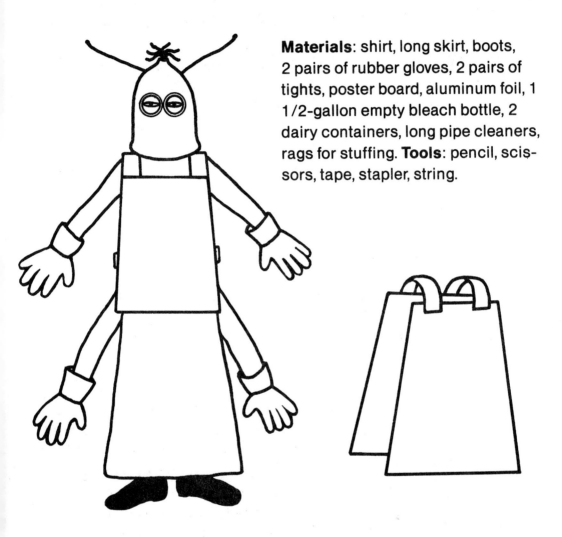

Materials: shirt, long skirt, boots, 2 pairs of rubber gloves, 2 pairs of tights, poster board, aluminum foil, 1 1/2-gallon empty bleach bottle, 2 dairy containers, long pipe cleaners, rags for stuffing. **Tools**: pencil, scissors, tape, stapler, string.

Vest

1. Cut 2 pieces of poster board. The top should measure the width of your chest, and the bottom should be 4 inches wider. The length should measure 4 inches below your waist.
2. Cut 4 poster board straps—1 1/2 inches wide and 12 inches long. Staple straps to attach the front to the back at the shoulders and sides.
3. Cover the vest with aluminum foil.

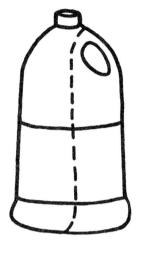

Second pair of arms

1. Stuff one leg of each pair of tights.
2. Tie gloves on the ends of the stuffed legs.

To wear arms, tie or pin the unstuffed legs around your waist.

Helmet

1. Cut the bottom and back off the bleach bottle. Cover the bottle with aluminum foil.
2. Cut round eye openings in the bottle. Be sure to fit it on your head before cutting.
3. Draw the outlines of the tops of dairy containers over eye holes. Cut slits in the outlines.
4. Cut tabs in the tops of the containers to fit the slits on the bottle. Cut out slits across the bottoms of the dairy containers.
5. Insert tabs in slits on bottle. Tape tabs down on the inside of the bottle.
6. Cut foil strips and stuff them into the neck of the bottle.
7. Attach foil tips to the ends of the pipe cleaners. Insert them on either side of the helmet. Tape bottom ends of pipe cleaners to the inside of the bottle.

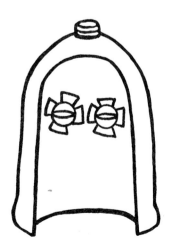

About the Author/Artist

Frieda Simone Gates studied art at the Brooklyn Museum Art School, The Art Students League, The New School for Social Research and New York University. Her paintings have been exhibited in New York City, Westchester and Rockland Counties. As a professional puppeteer, she performed with the Hudson Valley Vagabond Players. Currently, she is on the faculty of the art department at Rockland Community College. Mrs. Gates lives in Rockland County, New York, with her husband and their three children. This is her third book for Harvey House.